FROM SLAVES TO SOLDIERS

COMPILED BY JOANNE RANDOLPH

★

PowerKiDS
press

Published in 2018 by The Rosen Publishing Group, Inc.
29 East 21st Street, New York, NY 10010

"African Americans Enlist" by Judith Lee Hallock from Cobblestone Magazine (December 2002).
"Growing Up in Slavery" by Mike Weinstein and Marcia Amidon Lusted from Cobblestone Magazine (November 2011).
"African American Sailors" by Ruth Tenzer Feldman from Cobblestone Magazine (January 2004).
"Escape to Freedom" by Laura Phillips from Cobblestone Magazine (January 2004).

Cataloging-in-Publication Data

Names: Randolph, Joanne.
Title: From slaves to soldiers / compiled by Joanne Randolph.
Description: New York : PowerKids Press, 2018. | Series: The Civil War and Reconstruction: rebellion and rebuilding | Includes glossary and index.
Identifiers: LCCN ISBN 9781538340905 (pbk.) | ISBN 9781538340899 (library bound) | ISBN 9781538340912 (6 pack)
Subjects: LCSH: United States. Army--African American troops--History--19th century--Juvenile literature. | Slavery--Southern States--History--19th century--Juvenile literature. | African American soldiers--History--19th century--Juvenile literature. | United States--History--Civil War, 1861-1865--African Americans--Juvenile literature. | United States--History--Civil War, 1861-1865--Juvenile literature.
Classification: LCC E540.N3 F766 2018 | DDC 973.7'415--dc23

Designer: Katelyn E. Reynolds
Editor: Joanne Randolph

Photo credits: Cvr, p. 1 Kean Collection/Getty Images; cvr, pp. 1–32 (background texture) javarman/Shutterstock.com; cvr, pp. 1–32 (flags) cybrain/Shutterstock.com; cvr, pp. 1–32 (scroll) Seregam/Shutterstock.com; pp. 5, 6, 9, 10, 12, 14, 17, 21, 26, 28 courtesy of the Library of Congress; pp. 18, 27 © CORBIS/Corbis via Getty Images; p. 22 KudzuVine/Wikipedia.org (http://www.history.navy.mil/photos/images/h74000/h74054.jpg); p. 24 Hlj/Wikipedia.org (Map by Hal Jespersen, www.posix.com/CW).

Manufactured in the United States of America

CPSIA Compliance Information: Batch #CS18PK: For Further Information contact Rosen Publishing, New York, New York at 1-800-237-9932.

CONTENTS

WORDS IN THE GLOSSARY APPEAR
IN **BOLD** TYPE THE FIRST TIME
THEY ARE USED IN THE TEXT.

★

GROWING UP IN SLAVERY

The Civil War changed life for almost every American child living at that time. This was especially true for African American children who were born into slavery.

Young enslaved children were given jobs to do, like carrying water and picking up stones. They might work together as "trash gangs" to clean up yards or weed gardens. Children who were a little bit older could milk cows and feed chickens, or perhaps hold the master's horse for him whenever he wanted to go riding.

By the time enslaved children were 12, they were expected to do the same jobs that adults did. They might go into the fields to pick cotton or cultivate rice, as well as do any other job necessary for growing crops. Some children were trained to work in the "big house" where their master lived. They did chores, waited on family members, took care of their master's children, cleaned, and cooked.

THIS PHOTOGRAPH SHOWS
AN AFRICAN AMERICAN FAMILY IN FRONT
OF FORMER SLAVE QUARTERS AT
A PLANTATION IN SAVANNAH, GEORGIA.

THIS ILLUSTRATION FROM 1860 DEPICTS A SLAVE FATHER BEING SOLD AWAY FROM HIS FAMILY AT A SLAVE AUCTION.

Slaves were under the control of the people who "owned" them. Owners thought of these human beings as property. It was illegal for enslaved children to go to school or learn to read. They couldn't leave their farms or **plantations** without their owner's permission. Husbands, wives, and children could be sold away from each other at any time and possibly be separated forever. Enslaved children belonged to their master and not to their mother or father. Many did not even know their parents, because they had been separated from them. They had no freedom at all.

The Civil War was fought to **abolish** slavery. President Lincoln had freed the slaves who lived in the southern states when he issued the Emancipation Proclamation in 1863. As Union soldiers marched through the South, slaves escaped and fled to the camps of the Union army. Some rolled their few possessions into a blanket, took their children by the hand, and followed the Union soldiers. Many took up arms and joined in the fight that had given them their freedom.

AFRICAN AMERICANS ENLIST

By the end of the Civil War, the various U.S. armed forces had seen the services of nearly 200,000 African Americans. Some were free Northerners, some were escaped slaves, and some were former slaves who lived in areas taken over by Union forces. Although the North began accepting black **infantry** soldiers in 1862, it was late 1863 before the first black **cavalry regiments** were formed.

African Americans faced situations unlike those of other soldiers. Racial **prejudice** ran deep throughout America's white population. Many whites believed that blacks were too ignorant and cowardly to make good soldiers. But it did not take long for African American soldiers to prove their worth. Officers and fellow soldiers often praised the African Americans' performance on the battlefield. Northern white soldiers, once they fought next to black soldiers, came to accept them as valued partners.

SHOWN HERE IS A GROUP
OF SOLDIERS COMPRISED OF
BOTH BLACK AND WHITE MEN.

9

THIS PHOTOGRAPH SHOWS
AN AFRICAN AMERICAN SOLDIER
IN A UNION CAVALRY UNIFORM.

10

In December 1863, the first two regiments of African American cavalry, designated the 1st and 2nd U.S. Colored Cavalry (USCC), were organized in Virginia. They participated in combat operations as part of the force under Major General Benjamin Butler in eastern Virginia until the war ended. The 3rd USCC, created in March 1864, operated primarily out of Vicksburg, Mississippi. The 4th USCC, formed in New Orleans in April 1864, protected various sites in southern Louisiana. The 5th and 6th USCC were raised at Camp Nelson, Kentucky, in October 1864.

They were involved in various actions in Kentucky and southwestern Virginia. The experiences of the 5th USCC on a **campaign** in October 1864 illustrate what military service was like for many blacks. Recently recruited, the 5th was not yet fully organized, and most of its officers had not been appointed. The troops -- and their horses -- were poorly trained. Their weapons were infantry rifles, useless to soldiers on horseback. At first, the white soldiers with whom the African Americans marched ridiculed and insulted the black cavalrymen.

In this image, an African American regiment battles Confederate forces.

12

Union troops attacked an enemy line at Saltville, Virginia, on October 2. The Confederates became enraged when they saw the black units fighting against them, and so they targeted those cavalrymen. But the African Americans did not falter. A Union officer who earlier had expressed doubts about the blacks' fighting prowess admitted he "never saw troops fight like they did."

Another Northern officer reported, "I never saw any [soldiers] fight better." Ultimately, the Union army withdrew from Saltville, leaving behind their wounded. Some of the Confederate soldiers combed the battlefield and murdered the blacks who lay hurt and helpless.

"Our men took no negro prisoners," boasted a Confederate captain. A week later, several Southern soldiers forced their way into an army hospital and murdered any black soldiers they found there. When Confederate officers heard of these **atrocities**, they expressed outrage and sought to identify and punish those responsible.

This photograph from around 1898 shows African American soldiers on horseback during the Spanish-American War.

The Saltville battle shows the awful situation in which African Americans were placed when they tried to carry arms for their country. Many Southerners still looked upon them as slaves who needed to be "taught a lesson."

In December 1864, the 5th USCC returned to Saltville, in company with the 6th USCC and other cavalry. This time, they succeeded in destroying the local **saltworks**, depriving the Confederates of this precious **commodity**.

African Americans proved their worth throughout the Civil War, building a reputation as fine troopers who were courageous, able, and devoted. In 1866, when Congress scaled down the infantry, it provided for ten regiments of cavalry. Two of them, the 9th and 10th, were all black. These units saw service in the West, primarily "subduing" American Indians who attacked settlers trying to take over Indian land.

Despite continued prejudice, African American cavalrymen made significant contributions to the settlement of the West, just as they shared in the preservation of the Union during the Civil War.

AFRICAN AMERICAN SAILORS

Although African Americans had served in the U.S. Navy since the founding of the country, they were limited to five percent of monthly enlistments. At the start of the Civil War, however, the Union navy needed more men for its warships and so lifted this **quota**.

When Virginia seceded, slaves fled to that state's Fort Monroe, which was held by Union troops. The Northern commander there claimed that the slaves were **contraband**, and he refused to return them. Secretary of the Navy Gideon Welles decided to offer black contrabands the chance to enlist in the Union navy. Free African Americans also joined by the thousands.

Contraband sailors received ten dollars a month and the low rank of "boy." At a contraband's request, his salary could go to relatives living in Union navy–run contraband camps. Free African Americans enlisted at higher pay. Once in the navy, black sailors were ranked as landsmen, seamen, engineers, and pilots.

THIS PHOTOGRAPH OF
A YOUNG AFRICAN AMERICAN SAILOR
WAS TAKEN IN THE EARLY 1860S.

17

THIS PHOTOGRAPH SHOWS A GROUP OF AFRICAN AMERICAN SAILORS ABOARD THE USS VERMONT.

In general, African Americans in the Union navy got the same pay, benefits, and living quarters as white sailors of the same rank. The black enlisted men also enjoyed more civil rights than most states offered at the time. For duty during the Civil War, eight black sailors received the Medal of Honor for bravery, the highest military combat award any American can earn.

Estimates of the number of African Americans who served in the Union navy vary widely because sailors were not segregated or enlisted by race during the war. According to the Civil War Sailors Database (part of the Black Sailor Research Project at Howard University in Washington, D.C.), about 18,000 African Americans, including more than one dozen black women, were part of the Union navy during the Civil War – about fifteen percent of the total enlisted force.

Few records remain from the Confederate navy, and little is known about free African Americans or slaves who served on Confederate warships. Some were part of black gangs, referring to sailors (both black and white) who shoveled coal into the ships' engines. Others cooked or were servants to naval officers. A few free African Americans even enlisted as seamen. CSS *Chicora* is known to have had at least three.

ESCAPE TO FREEDOM

On May 13, 1862, just outside Charleston Harbor, South Carolina, the Union naval commander of the USS *Onward* was about to give the order to fire on an armed Confederate steamship heading his way. Then he noticed a white flag of surrender on the steamer's mast. The pilot of the boat was an enslaved African American named Robert Smalls, who was attempting to escape by stealing the Confederate ship!

Smalls was born into slavery on April 5, 1839, in Beaufort, South Carolina. By the time he was 12 years old, his master began to hire him out to do various jobs in Charleston. Smalls eventually worked at the docks, learning how to make sails and paint ships. He also learned how to read nautical maps. Over time, he became an excellent sailor and navigator. He could steer any ship through narrow waterways without running into rocks.

ROBERT SMALLS

ROBERT SMALLS escaped CHARLESTON HARBOR
on the CONFEDERATE transport ship
CSS *PLANTER*.

SMALLS AND OTHER ENSLAVED CREWMEMBERS ABOARD THE CSS *Planter* ATTEMPTED THEIR ESCAPE ON MAY 13, 1862.

In 1861, Smalls was working on a 150-foot steamboat called the *Planter*. The powerful steamer had been turned into a Confederate army ferry and supply gunboat. It was the fastest vessel in the harbor and, as such, was the most important ship in the local Southern fleet.

Since April 1861, the Southern army had held Fort Sumter, a large defensive island fort at the mouth of Charleston Harbor. Beyond the harbor was a blockade of Northern ships. Smalls and his wife, Hannah, dreamed of escaping from slavery and raising their two children in freedom. Smalls believed that he and his family might be free if they could make it to the blockade.

In the early morning hours of May 13, the *Planter*'s three white officers left the ship to spend the night ashore. Seizing the opportunity, Smalls and the majority of the other enslaved crewmembers set an escape plan in motion. They decided to steal the ship, but they agreed that if anything went wrong, they would blow it up to avoid capture.

CHARLESTON
HARBOR

FORT
JOHNSON

FORT
SUMTER

The crew fired up the boat's boilers and set off. Smalls first picked up his family and the families of the other crewmen from a nearby wharf. With nine men, five women, and three children aboard, the *Planter* headed toward the mouth of the harbor.

As the ship passed by Fort Johnson near the southern shore of the harbor, Smalls gave the secret signal – two long pulls followed by one short pull on the whistle cord – and the sentry let the steamer pass. He put on the broad-brimmed straw hat that belonged to the *Planter*'s captain. Disguised that way, he again gave the signal and was allowed to steam past Fort Sumter. Eager to get out of range of the fort's guns, he increased the ship's speed for the last three miles.

When Smalls pulled alongside the *Onward*, he announced to the commander that he was returning "some of your U.S. guns, sir." The *Planter* proved to be a great prize for the North. The vessel could travel in shallower waters than most other ships. Smalls gave Admiral Samuel Francis Du Pont, the Union commander of the blockade, a book he had managed to steal that contained all the secret signals and codes of the Confederate navy.

AFRICAN AMERICAN SOLDIERS
JOIN THE STORMING OF FORT WAGNER
IN SOUTH CAROLINA.

Upon hearing the story of Smalls's escape from slavery, a writer at *The New York Times* declared the deed to be "one of the most heroic acts of the war." If they had been caught, the punishment would have been severe. Smalls and his fellow crewmembers were awarded the prize money for the Confederate vessel.

Smalls also shared valuable information about South Carolina's waterways with the Union navy. He had memorized the location, size, and strength of Confederate fortifications along the coast. He knew where torpedoes and mines had been placed in the water. Soon, he was given a job as the *Planter*'s pilot.

Smalls's actions introduced him to important men. In a meeting with President Abraham Lincoln and Secretary of War Edwin M. Stanton in August 1862, he convinced them that African Americans could make an important contribution to the war effort. Smalls helped raise 5,000 volunteers, who later formed two South Carolina infantry regiments that fought for the Union.

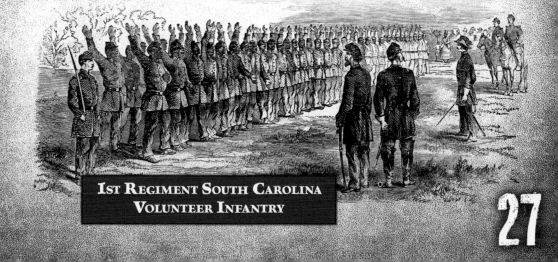

1st Regiment South Carolina Volunteer Infantry

ROBERT SMALLS, SHOWN HERE,
SERVED AS A U.S. CONGRESSMAN,
REPRESENTING SOUTH CAROLINA.

In December 1863, Smalls was promoted to captain of the *Planter*. He became the first black captain of a vessel in the service of the United States, for which he earned $150 a month. He piloted the *Planter* and the USS *Keokuk* along the South Carolina and Georgia coasts for the rest of the war. During that time, Smalls was in 17 engagements, and he was present in Charleston Harbor in April 1865 when Union forces resumed control of Fort Sumter. He returned to Beaufort after the war, where he bought his former master's home and started several businesses.

Robert Smalls was among the first generation of African Americans to become active in politics. He won election to the South Carolina legislature and to five terms in the U.S. House of Representatives, where he fought for the rights of black citizens. He died in 1915.

GLOSSARY

abolish: Get rid of.

atrocities: Appalling conditions or behaviors.

campaign: A series of military actions that are designed to achieve a certain purpose, usually in a certain area or using a particular kind of fighting.

cavalry: Soldiers who fight on horseback.

commodity: A raw material or major agricultural product that can be bought and sold.

contraband: Enemy property seized to deny its benefits to enemy troops.

infantry: Soldiers that fight on foot.

plantation: An estate on which crops such as tobacco, sugar, and coffee are grown by resident workers.

prejudice: Dislike, hostility, or unfair treatment based on unfounded opinions that are not based on reason or real experience.

quota: The maximum number that may be admitted to a group or institution.

regiment: A permanent unit of an army that is often under the control of a colonel and may be subdivided into several smaller squadrons or units.

saltworks: A place where salt is produced.

FOR MORE INFORMATION

BOOKS

Ford, Carin T. *African-American Soldiers in the Civil War: Fighting for Freedom*. New York: Enlsow Publishing, 2004.

Lanier, Wendy. *What Was the Missouri Compromise?: And Other Questions About the Struggle over Slavery*. New York: Lerner Publishing, 2012.

Reis, Ronald A., and Tim McNeese. *African Americans and the Civil War*. New York: Chelsea House Publications, 2009.

WEBSITES

Black Soldiers in the U.S. Military During the Civil War
https://www.archives.gov/education/lessons/blacks-civil-war

Black Civil War Soldiers
http://www.history.com/topics/american-civil-war/black-civil-war-soldiers

INDEX